FARM ANIMALS

COW

Katie Dicker

W
FRANKLIN WATTS
LONDON•SYDNEY

 An Appleseed Editions book

Franklin Watts
First published in Great Britain in 2017
by The Watts Publishing Group

Created by Appleseed Editions Ltd,
Well House, Friars Hill, Guestling,
East Sussex TN35 4ET

Designed by Hel James
Edited by Mary-Jane Wilkins

ISBN hardback 978 1 4451 5091 8
Dewey Classification 626.2

A CIP catalogue for this book is available from the British Library

Photo acknowledgements
l = left, r = right, t = top, b = bottom
title page Eric Isselée/Shutterstock, page 3 smereka/Shutterstock, 5 Digital Vision/
Thinkstock; 6 val lawless/Shutterstock; 7 Hemera/Thinkstock; 8 Niels Quist/
Shutterstock; 9t aodaodaodaod, b Dmitry Kalinovsky/both Shutterstock; 10
Monkey Business Images/Shutterstock; 11 Igorsky/Shutterstock; 12 David Maska/
Shutterstock; 13 Hemera/Thinkstock; 14 Christian Musat/Shutterstock;
15 iStockphoto/Thinkstock; 16 Wasan Srisawat/Shutterstock; 17 iStockphoto/
Thinkstock; 18 digitalreflections/Shutterstock; 19t tepic, b TFoxFoto/both
Shutterstock; 20t Ewan Chesser, b Malgorzata Kistryn/both Shutterstock;
21t Andresr, b James Laurie/both Shutterstock; 22 Dorling Kindersley RF/
Thinkstock; 23 iStockphoto/Thinkstock
Cover Dudarev Mikhail/Shutterstock

Printed in China

Franklin Watts
An imprint of Hachette Children's Group
Part of The Watts Publishing Group
Carmelite House
50 Victoria Embankment
London EC4Y 0DZ

An Hachette UK Company
www.hachette.co.uk

www.franklinwatts.co.uk

tents

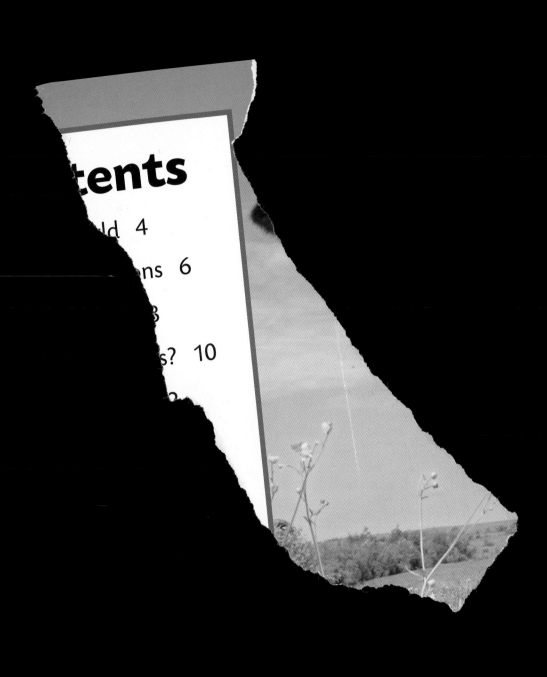

world

ve on a dairy fa
of other cow
some of my

mmer, we live out
raze on grass in th

Con...

arm
vs.
herd.

doors.
e fields.

**Cows graze
for up to eight
hours a day.**

Moooo!

Changing seasons

In the hot sun, we rest in the shade of trees in the pasture.

Cows don't sleep for long, but they like a comfortable spot to rest.

In winter, we shelter in the barn.
The straw helps to keep us warm.

Top to toe

A cow's long tail can swipe at irritating insects.

Swishhh!

Most cows have a coat of black, brown or white hair.

We can walk through slippery mud or over rough stones with our strong hoofs.

Some male and female cows have horns.

Who looks after us?

Our spacious barn is warm and dry. The farmer keeps it clean and makes sure we have enough to eat.

A vet visits regularly to keep us healthy and clip our hoofs.

This feeder is full of clean hay for us to eat.

Time to eat

Munch!

Our favourite foods are grass, hay and leaves. In winter, we eat cereals and vitamins too.

I move my head to tear leaves from the ground. A long tongue helps me chew.

Cows and calves

Dairy cows have a baby, called a calf,
once a year. A bull is used to breed them.

Slurp

Newborn calves drink
their mother's milk.
Some calves are bottle-fed.

A young calf
drinks about
4.5 litres of
milk every day.

The milking parlour

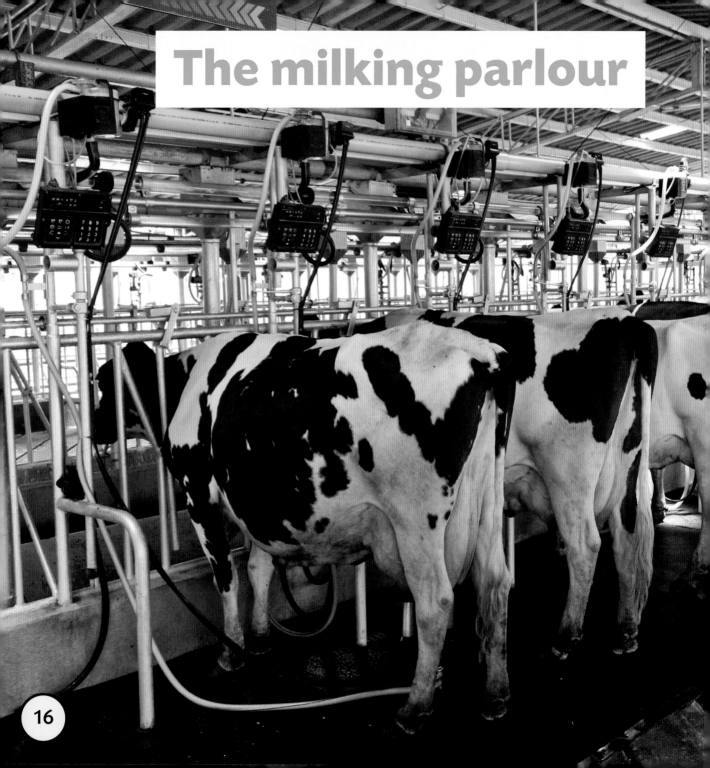

We go to the milking parlour twice a day. The farmer puts milking machines on our udders.

The milk is stored in a cold tank before trucks take it away to be sold.

In the past, cows were milked by hand.

Dairy cows make up to 22 litres of milk every day!

Farm produce

Cows are farmed for their milk, meat and leather. Their milk is used to make dairy products, such as butter, cheese and yogurt.

Herefords are bred for their meat, called beef.

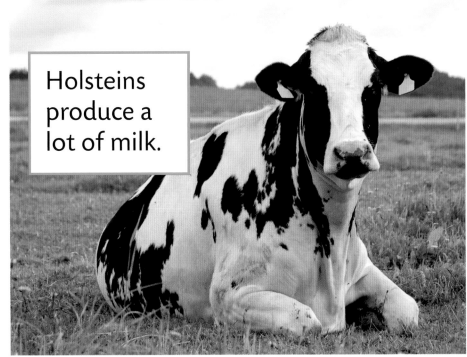

Holsteins produce a lot of milk.

Jersey cows are smaller, but their milk is creamier.

Cows around the world

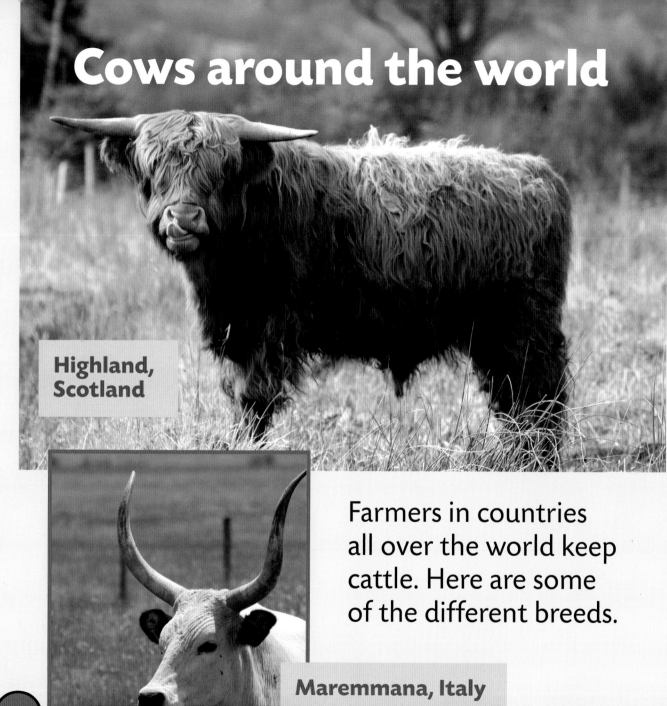

Highland, Scotland

Farmers in countries all over the world keep cattle. Here are some of the different breeds.

Maremmana, Italy

Zebu, India

Long ago, farmers kept cows for both their milk and their meat. Today, most farmers keep either dairy cattle or beef cattle.

Texas Longhorn, USA

Did you know?

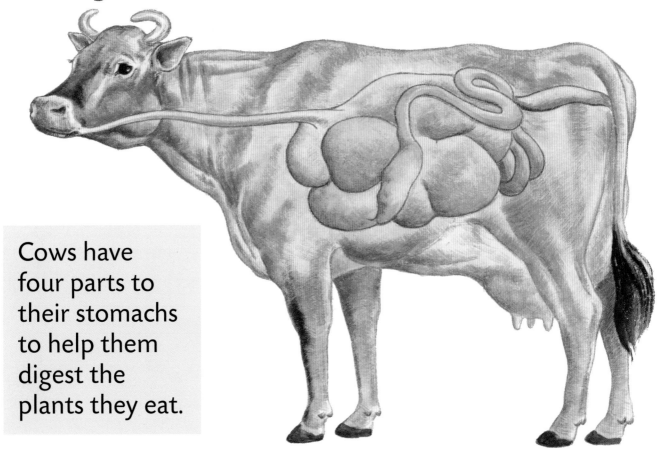

Cows have four parts to their stomachs to help them digest the plants they eat.

A cow has no top teeth at the front of its mouth.

Dairy cows need to drink lots of water: up to 227 litres a day – that's about a bathtub full!

A cow moves its jaw and tongue up to 60,000 times a day to chew its food. All that chewing makes about 114 litres of saliva.

Useful words

bull
A male cow.

graze
Animals graze when they eat grass.

herd
A group of animals that live together.

leather
A material made from the skin of an animal.

pasture
Land used for grazing.

Index

barn 7, 10
beef 18, 19, 21
breeds 18, 19, 20, 21
bulls 14, 23

calves 14, 15

food 4, 10, 11, 12, 13,
  15, 22, 23

herd 4, 23
hoofs 9, 10

horns 9

milk 15, 16, 17, 18, 19, 21

sleeping 6
stomachs 22

tail 8
teeth 22
tongue 13, 23

vet 10

Websites

www.animalcorner.co.uk/farm/cows/cow_about.html
www.sites.ext.vt.edu/virtualfarm/dairy/dairy.html
www.moomilk.com
http://www.ciwf.org.uk/farm-animals/cows/dairy-cows/
http://kidcyber.com.au/topics/animals/cattle/